Stephen Clarke

Bill Home.

Published in 2007 by
Surrealist Editions
6 Aberdeen Grove
Leeds LS12 3QY

© Stephen J. Clark 2007
© Bill Howe 2007

ISBN 978-1-906238-01-8

Printed in Great Britain by
Beamreach Printing, Liversedge, West Yorkshire

The Bridge of
Shadows

Poems by Stephen J. Clark
&
Photographs by Bill Howe

Surrealist Editions

"From her (Nature) there preceded many heads without necks, arms wandered about by themselves without shoulders, and eyes floated in mid-air without faces."

- Empedocles

The Bridge of Shadows

The Other Side (Treatise)

Speech steals
from shadows

where sight is in love
with the end of itself

the world rolls lost
in an ever-dilating gaze

a vocabulary of absence
that promises everything

its trembling roots
a moth's antennae

caressing the elsewhere
of everything

what can it not contain
yet Nothing is its name

it is time
hidden

behind closed lips

another life lives
secretly words

walk wild
while mouths are sleeping

Transfusion

Break the bread of speech
on these lost paths

love the thunder
the whispered thunder
has unwritten me

in you my breath
will sing through bone

in you my blood
will find no rest

nor will you
my fear sleep in me

break the bread of speech

Nursery Song

Dangerously small hands

insects

across the eons the eons

swarming

on bridges falling

down

through stars sand skin

bone

their home

a head of nevers

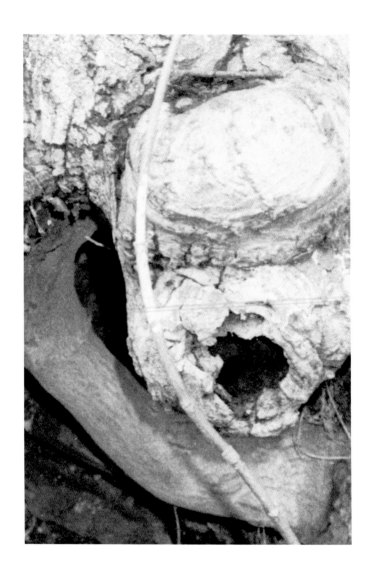

Infant Void

Vertiginous furniture looms over you
as breath about to fall

a pulse softly drums
along a cord
that begins and ends
in shadow

a murmur in Morse

waiting for another sound
an ardent star of human bone

a fist closing on a fist closing on a fist

waiting for another sound
a vegetal door of human glass

where Nothing is impenetrable

footprints run away
tapping
across the frozen air
blackened by artificial light

above a distant floor
of restless feathers

one white footprint falling

where Nothing is impenetrable

Physiognomy

The whole body as a key
its head turning in the lock
of unknown hours
from which ash falls
to form the walls of a room
where bodies in corners
with faces of thread
reach out their luminous fingers
to unravel their brothers' heads
finding the air
a labyrinth of answers.

The Bridge of Shadows

The abyss smiles

undressed it will know me
embowed bone
on strings   noosed limbs

hands climbing up lips
hungry swarm of Braille
topographies converge
on the descendent
stairwell
that unwinds
the sound of naked feet

maps shrink
to pattern a shattered glass
spying as quiet as pitch

is this the place
that you told me
never existed

is this the place
where the abyss
will lose itself
in the crowd
of a mouth made
from cracking skin
crumbling around
an ever-deforming jaw
whose many voices
call on distant words
to shape us

into the dark ahead

how will we greet strangers
resist secrets
beyond hearing
who will we speak of
space without memory
it is you
you can never hold

never escape

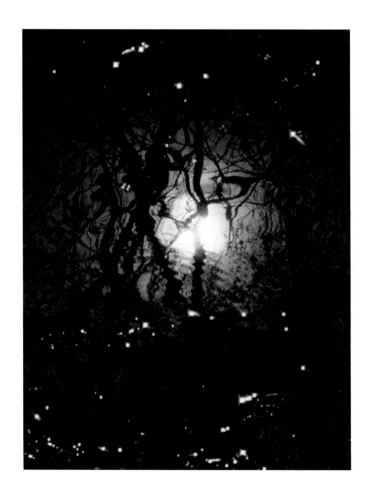

Conditions

What what it is
to walk the stairs at night
on bare black boards

a seismographic finger
trembling with equations

your voice has stormed
these etched paths

so easily erased

your voice unheard
thunder asleep

beyond this turbulence

lies nothing   no word
no breath   no bone
to flesh   no thread
to lose   no ink

lingering thought to Night

Hourglass

This head remembered
emptied its voice
drained down
a glass throat

The dead
take turns
at living

one mouth buried
so another can open

every grain that falls
each word breathed

widens the desert
of permanent exhalation

pouring loss
the lips of our cup
encircle utter silence

Homunculus Drunk

We share a spine
in the turning void
we divide our time
under burning soil
inside one skull
our features dance
convulsed in flame
the distance laughs
as it falls away
into the distance laughing
as it falls away
one hand clapping
deforming clay
into the distance laughing
as it falls away

We sink a knife
into our drunken voice
tear out tongues
to croon our songs
red clay shaped
by our blackened thumbs
silence reclaims
the distance laughs
as it falls away
into the distance laughing
as it falls away
one tongue lapping
this stolen air
into the distance laughing
as it falls away

21

Polyphemus

Eye eat out the I
whose throne resides
within the jewel

where it holds court
with compound eyes

staring at once
through every facet
feasting

at once I will be there
the great in the small

a pretender to the Invisible

tomorrow returned
in a glance

who will I keep in my pockets

Nobody

that is my name

an insect devouring angels eating gods

Nobody

that is not my name!

Golem

Hand shapes hand
opens to close
your kiss
bites out my mouth
you taste the clay
of my tongue

night thumbs
our lids
light our eyes
blinded
by burning names

I build my labyrinth
in your ear
I vein your hair
you heel my heart
you eat your words
to end my voice

Unknowable

The bulb has been stroked
black from within

a single 'I' of Morse code
taps in the corrugated dark

between telling and understanding
memory hums out of tune

who will rouse it
from its silent exits
when the body disobeys

and the mouth
that wouldn't close
made of imagined bone
utters a name dissolving
in the ink of eyes

as wide as the unseen
unravelling moons
in the corners of rooms
the body disobeys
the sigils of the dead
that mark the mouth
that wouldn't close

In Absentia

A mouth speaking backwards
the immeasurable instant
witness to a kiss
that pinioned
the first bird
of the coming storm

all is prepared tonight
as in a theatre
or final breath

what toys
what Braille
the morning rain leaves

glass accents suspended
everything depends
on how you will fall
how the beads broken
from this abacus
will cease to roll

again the sea
combs your face
into the shoreline

and unearths stones
scarred with radiant ciphers
stars that stride
across each brow

the bird will make
a garden of your jaw

plume of bone
gesture thousands of years
in accomplishment

a searching dissolution
in your arabesques
immensity

a fontanelle of smoke
between each jolt of the eye

unmade and on the verge
of making you
on the other side of skin

this violence of sound
world enflamed
movement that is fear
beauty only before
it is torn away
torn into distances

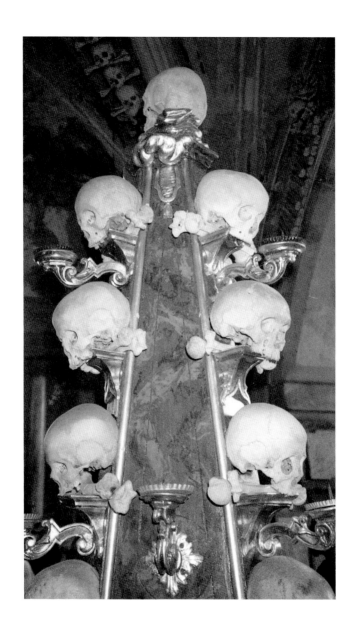

Homesickness

The sound of the air
tearing inside rooms
behind the rooms remembered

where the glass
has forgotten
how to build
my reflection

twin you have
taken my voice

tunnelled you have
crawled your way
into the belly
of my bed

through ugly peepholes
that sleep gnawed

coiled inside
a nude bell

this child
of the dawn

dreaming a nervous system

Anaesthesia

Human confetti
reluctant food
for a shadow's gravity
that words wounds
to be opened again
in this body between us

this theatre of strangers

a crowd of one
its bread our bones
under all possible cutlery
yet to take seed
on our tongue its table
for a silent feast

Sweet Nothings

1.
Little man
you have marked
in secret
a silver face
to see if you
may one day find
that same face
in your hand
again

2.
Her face
white bell inverted
doll tolling
doll swallowing
sound
and this boy
whose voice didn't break

3.
Bird of thread
the forest soon
unravels what
you cannot trace
your knot a frown
undone a smile

a skipping rope around the abyss

Infusorian

Upon entrance
you will lose your way
all your nights
born at once

you become ink
that never dries
but crawls beneath
a firmament sealed
by Titan hands
above division

without walls
you feed on thread
that brings
only hunger

silence

how you long
to be invited

perhaps your labyrinth
moving in mine
will never agree
doors will not find doors
in this city of wheels

The Late Guest

To find you there
in a Rorschach coat

dressed in white evening
where the garden recedes

awaiting the X-ray
after the dream

drunk on light
when the darkness bleeds

blue is this sleep
of everything

is this sleep
the falling to sleep
of everything

the falling to sleep
of sound

the sound of blood

and the first morning of childhood

Afterwords

The Other Side (Treatise) Part II

Poetry is a way of understanding and experiencing. What we hide and what we deny are also part of the way we speak and see. Language and sight constitute a dialogue of attraction and repulsion. Words and images conflict and make love, they may unite to form patterns that are seductively receptive to our desire to understand, or destroy each other, interrupting, unravelling and questioning in a game where our world of meaning and experience is at risk. An insect could devour the world in one night.

In poetic experience our enervated senses are at play in the realm of the possible, where we are drawn into associative constellations, where we become leaping words and falling silences. Discoveries are not observed at a distance. We are immersed in our looking, soluble in our reading and in our doing so, we experience a turbulent communion, becoming conspirators inextricably part of a world that confides secrets we struggle to comprehend. The impressions and perceptions that we form and project return to us transformed by the object of our attention. These returning perspectives of the object take possession of us as a double, a Doppelgänger. Mesmerised, we recognise ourselves there but not as we had expected, engaged in reciprocal inspiration with phenomena.

Poetry makes the volatile stable and the stable volatile. In this exchange our world never rests but is perpetually transformed. In this creative process the world is in flux, is all ripples, furrows and lacunae. Stone becomes water. The entire garden is blown away with its petals, and light is defined by shadow. It is the silent, dreamt, lost, useless, decaying and broken that can further inform our experiences and memories of time and space in developing a consistent, if vulnerable, poetic understanding that we might otherwise neglect. Or if it is not an understanding, then it is a sense of wonder, fear or loss that is ecstatic. It is this complex play of associations, of language and seeing, of absence and presence, that makes us what we are and makes us part of what we are not.

Stephen J. Clark

Prospecting For The Marvellous

"We have been expelled from the centre of the world and are condemned to search for it through jungles and deserts or in the underground mazes of the labyrinth."

Octavio Paz - *The Labyrinth of Solitude*

A grey day, miserable with showers, shuddering out of doors, sheltering under eaves and in doorways, one eye on the clouds, as if to gauge when the rainfall will stop. Shafts of sunlight slanting into the grass, on the other side of the dry stone wall, perpetually chewing, indifferent sheep, go about their mundane business. A breach in the castle wall at Middleham, seat of Richard the hunchback. A moment of no significance, one interval marked only by a click of the finger, unremembered in the multiplicity of other things occuring that seemed to be of more importance on that day. The images accrue significance in their journey away from the experience – by revisitation, re-revelation of experiences. But you were not with us on these expeditions, conducting instead your own experiments in the crucible of life. So we play a game of sharing, leaving trails for you to follow, to wander along and get lost.

The images presented here may offer some resonances, relationships, echoes, reverberations and correlations, but these are essentially for the reader to discover and reveal. Images are transformed into objects. A collection of poems and photographs that becomes an object which can itself be rediscovered and interrogated, a game of creative exploration of the interrelationships between poem and photograph.

So here is evidence, fragments left over from experience, shadows, traces of powerful moments distilled, magnified, framed, frozen. Evidence of the marvellous. The photographs themselves are not illustrations, interpretations or explanations, not substitutes for words. Conceived as self-contained, gathered as evidence of poetic revelation, collected at different times and places, this temporary companionship of images and texts, combined by entirely subjective processes, allows the forming of new interrelationships, new experiences. A process of discovery and revelation, analogous to the physical process of producing the photographic prints. The dialectic between silence and speech, moment and memory, between the photographic 'negative' and the 'positive' print. Humming with the heartbeat of this dialectic, past and future are synthesised in the present.

The image is a record of possibilities, the shadows cast by past events wheel around the sundial, pointing clearly towards what is possible, a peeling back of the skin of the world to reveal something essential below the surface, subjective experience becomes the source of meaning, of the marvellous, of the essence of life. The poetic instant.

Bill Howe

Printed in a limited edition of 350 copies

of which this is number ...19....